Grandmother's Adobe Dollhouse

by MaryLou M. Smith

Illustrated by Ann Blackstone

New Mexico Magazine • Santa Fe

A special **muchas gracias** to Ann Marie Bottoms.

Copyright ©1984 by MaryLou M. Smith.
All rights reserved.
Printed in the United States of America.
First Edition
Published by
NEW MEXICO MAGAZINE:
A Nuevo West Book

Library of Congress Cataloging in Publication Data
Smith, MaryLou M., 1950–
Grandmother's Adobe Dollhouse.
Summary: A young boy describes his grandmother's adobe dollhouse giving information about the architecture, art, food, and culture of New Mexico.
1. Dollhouses — New Mexico — Juvenile literature.
2. Dollhouses — Collectors and collecting — New Mexico — Juvenile literature. 3. New Mexico — Social life and customs — Juvenile literature. [1. Dollhouses. 2. New Mexico — Social life and customs. 3. Collectors and collecting.] I. Blackstone, Ann, ill. II. Title. III. Title: Grandmother's adobe doll house.
NK4894.U6S65 1984 745.592'3'09789 84-91156
ISBN 0-937-206-03-2

▧ Preface

Many of the words about my grandmother's dollhouse are Spanish, and you will want to learn how to say them. Grandmother and I wrote a "helper" after each Spanish word, to explain how to say it.

You will be glad you took time to learn to say the words the way they are supposed to be said. Each word about each part of my grandmother's adobe dollhouse sounds just like it was made to fit!

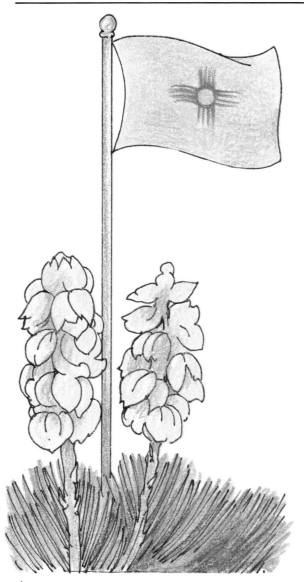

My grandmother lives in New Mexico. She loves dollhouses and all the things you put inside them. My favorite one is her adobe dollhouse. When Grandmother and I play with her adobe dollhouse, she tells me all about New Mexico.

Grandmother made her dollhouse to look just like a real New Mexican adobe house. She traveled all over New Mexico to collect the tiny things inside.

Grandmother says there are no houses in the world like the adobe houses in New Mexico. She says they were made by the hands of the people of New Mexico: the Pueblo Indians, the Navajo Indians, and the Spanish colonists. And the early Anglo settlers, and the Mexican settlers, too. That's a lot of hands!

Let me show you around Grandmother's adobe dollhouse and you will see what I mean.

Follow me, but be sure to walk on your fingertips. Let's pretend we are only three inches tall. Things that are one foot tall in a regular house are only one inch tall in Grandmother's dollhouse.

See the string of red chiles hanging outside the front door to dry? Grandmother calls that a **ristra** [REE-strah]. Every time I see a ristra I want to pull off one of the bright red chiles and eat it. But Grandmother says they are hot enough to burn my tongue.

We have to wait until the chiles have dried. Then she will grind up just one chile to put into enchiladas for supper. I don't mind waiting. Grandmother's enchiladas are delicious!

Before we go in, let me tell you about **adobe** [ah-DOH-beh]. This little house and all the adobe houses in New Mexico are really made of mud.

The Pueblo Indians made their houses out of adobe mud a long, long time ago. They shaped the mud into walls with their hands.

When the Spanish came to New Mexico, everybody started making the adobe mud into bricks. They stacked the bricks to make walls.

If you want to make an adobe house, you must first dig clay soil out of the ground. Then mix the soil with water and stir it around, just as if you were making mud pies. You can add some straw to keep the adobe from cracking when it dries.

Now pile the mud into some wide wooden molds, and smooth it over. Put your bricks out in the bright New Mexico sun, and when they are dry they will be hard enough to build a house.

I have never made adobe bricks, but it seems to me you would need a friend to help. Should we try it someday?

Now that we're inside, don't you want to look everywhere at once?

Look up above your head. See the ceiling made of sticks? Those sticks are called **latillas** [lah-TEE-yahs]. They are really little saplings from trees.

The beams are called **vigas** [VEE-gahs]. They hold up the adobe roof.

See the way the latillas are laid in between the vigas first one way and then the other? Grandmother says that gives them a "herring-bone" effect. I like the way the sticks snuggle up close to one another.

Those carved blocks at the end of each viga are called **corbels.** Don't they make the vigas look tidy at the ends? Sometimes the corbels are plain, and sometimes they are fancy.

Later, when we go back outside, be sure to look up on the sides of the house. You will see the vigas sticking out through the adobe walls.

One of Grandmother's books says that the Pueblo Indians first made vigas that stuck out that way. The logs they made the vigas out of did not always fit just right, so they let them stick out. I think that was a smart way to handle the problem. Do you?

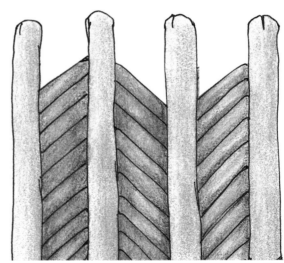

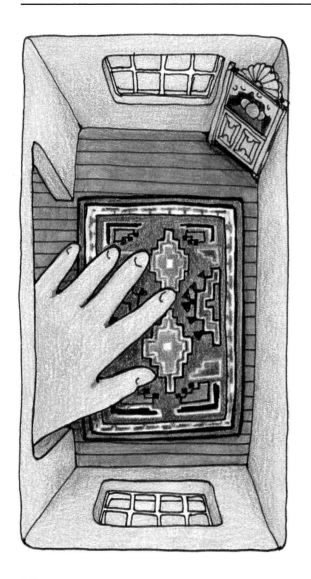

Now, look down, below your fingertips.

Can you believe someone's hands could make such a tiny rug with such beautiful designs? Grandmother traveled to Northern New Mexico to meet the woman who made that rug.

She is a Navajo Indian, and she made this tiny rug to look just like the blankets her people have been making for many years.

First they shear the wool from the sheep they tend. Then they spin the wool into yarn and weave it on up-and-down looms.

This little rug is called a **Two Gray Hills rug.** One day I looked and looked trying to find the gray hills. Then Grandmother told me that Two Gray Hills is the name of the trading post near where the rug is made. That's where the two gray hills are!

You can tell a Two Gray Hills rug by its colors. For this rug, the Navajos use the wool just as it comes from the sheep, without adding any other colors.

Some of their sheep have black wool, and some have white. All the different shades of brown in their rugs come from their brown sheep.

I like to close my eyes and imagine the Navajo shepherds walking over those gray hills tending their sheep of many colors.

Let's go to the kitchen. I have lots of things to show you there.

Open your hand and close your eyes. Now open your eyes. See the tiny green **chiles** [CHEE-lehs]? I got them off the tiled counter over there. They are just like the real ones we have at Grandmother's house at almost every meal.

You may think that green chiles are very, very hot, but Grandmother says there are many varieties. She buys the mild ones just for me.

Sometimes she lets me help her roast them in the oven until we see brown blisters where the bright green used to be. Then we quickly dunk them in ice cold water. When we peel off the brown blistery part they are bright green again underneath.

Grandmother stuffs the chiles with cubes of cheese while I beat up the eggs. Then when everyone is hungry she dips the chiles in the eggs and cooks them in hot oil.

After that, I hurry quickly to the table where everyone is waiting. I don't want to miss out on my share!

See those ears of corn in that tiny basket? Some people call it **Indian corn.** I was surprised to find out corn could be blue or brown or even red! My favorite is the one with yellow and brown kernels all in the same ear.

Grandmother says that nowadays most people just use this corn to make their kitchens look cheerful. Sometimes they hang it on the wall and sometimes they put it in baskets. They do their cooking with more modern varieties of corn.

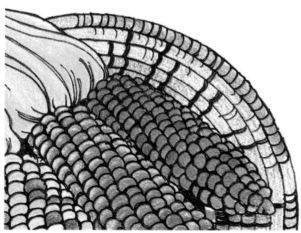

But I'd like to try to cook with this corn. We could try to make my Grandmother's **posole** [poh-SO-leh]. Have you ever eaten any?

The best thing about posole is how it smells when you come in the house. It's made with hominy. They used to have to make hominy out of corn that had been soaked in lye. But now Grandmother buys the hominy at the grocery store in a package next to the packages of dried red chiles.

First she soaks it in water. Then she cooks it with pork and pods of red chile, and lots of garlic and onions.

I like posole. Grandmother lets me dip my tortilla into the bowl so I won't miss even one juicy bit.

Have you ever seen a bed in a kitchen? Well, look over there. That fireplace in the corner with the long flat shelf on top is called a **shepherd's bed.** Some people call it a **shepherd's fireplace.**

At first I thought Grandmother was making up a funny story when she told me shepherds used to sleep up on that shelf. The fire underneath kept them warm.

Really, anybody could sleep there, but mostly it was a place for drying chiles and squash and other things to eat.

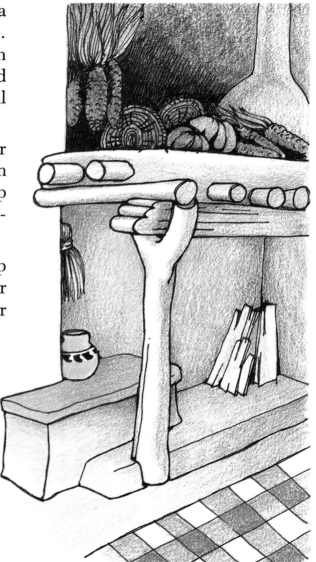

Are you thirsty? Let's pretend those pretty pots near the window have water in them. The Spanish named them **ollas** [OH-yahs].

Grandmother says the Pueblo Indians first made the ollas to carry their water in. The women can carry the pots on their heads without any hands.

Ollas are made out of long fat snakes of clay coiled around and around. Then the pots are smoothed so carefully you can't believe they ever looked like snakes. Grandmother says it takes a long time and the Indians do not hurry.

See the different patterns and shapes painted on the outside? Each pueblo or village has its own special designs and colors.

The Indians paint the designs with brushes made out of the stringy fibers of a yucca plant. And they make different colors of paint out of plants and minerals they find outside.

Do you know what Grandmother told me about the black designs on these ollas? They were painted with a thick syrup made from a Rocky Mountain bee plant. The Indians boil the leafy stems in water to make a paint that looks like black licorice.

Grandmother promises that someday she and I can try to make pots with clay. We might even try to make our own paint. Would you like to help us?

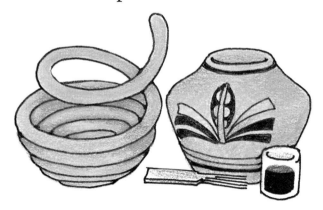

Let's go back to the living room. I have lots more things to show you there.

This fireplace is called a **Santa Fe fireplace.** It's made of adobe clay too, just like the walls.

And look, even some of the furniture in this house is made of clay. Benches like these are called **bancos** [BAHN-cohs]. They can be straight against the wall or curve around corners.

Those cubbyholes in the wall above the fireplace are made when the adobe walls are being built. Grandmother calls them **nichos** [NEE-chohs].

I like the way the bancos and the nichos and the Santa Fe fireplace look like they were all made out of the same piece of adobe clay.

Do you like dolls as much as I do? Well, Grandmother has some made out of clay. If we are very careful we can hold them.

See all the little children cuddled around their grandfather? I like the way some are on his lap and some are on his legs and some are even up on his shoulders. Grandmother calls him a **storyteller.** She says each storyteller is a little different but the storyteller's mouth is always open because he's singing.

The Indians from Cochiti Pueblo made Grandmother's storytellers. Don't the children look happy? They remind me of how I feel when Grandmother says to me, "Matt, why don't you come sit in my lap and I'll tell you a story."

This little statue is made out of wood. It is called a **bulto** [BOOHL-toh]. Bultos are carved religious figures that the Spanish Colonists made when they came to New Mexico many years ago.

Sometimes the religious figures are painted on a flat piece of wood. Then they are called **retablos** [reh-TAH-blohs]. Did you see the one in the corner above the bancos?

A name often used for either a retablo or a bulto is **santo** [SAHN-toh]. Very talented carvers and painters called **santeros** [sahn-TEH-rohs] made them.

I'm glad Grandmother keeps the storyteller and the bulto safely tucked away in the nichos.

Let's go upstairs now. Bet I can beat you!

Isn't this dollhouse full of fireplaces? The one in the corner of this bedroom is called a **beehive fireplace.**

A beehive fireplace looks a lot like the outdoor ovens the Pueblo Indians bake their bread in. The Spanish just moved them indoors and made fireplaces out of them.

This smooth wooden cabinet is called a **trastero** [trahs-TEH-roh]. Here in the bedroom it takes the place of a closet to hold clothes. But usually people put trasteros in the kitchen to hold dishes and other kitchen things.

Mexican cabinet makers called **carpinteros** [cahr-peen-TEH-rohs] came to New Mexico to build trasteros and other pieces of carved wooden furniture.

Grandmother says that in those days, a New Mexico family's most special piece of furniture was their trastero.

I like to pretend the sun is shining through the little squares of glass in these **French doors.** I asked Grandmother if these French doors came from France. I couldn't figure out how an adobe house in New Mexico got doors like these.

Grandmother told me that the French doors came from the early Anglo settlers. When they came to New Mexico they got homesick for the kind of furniture they had back East. So they sent home for doors and chairs and sofas like they were used to. Some of it came to New Mexico on big trains.

If you want to open one of the tiny doors we can go outside.

Now look where we are. This is the upstairs **patio** [PAH-tee-oh].

At Christmastime we line up **luminarias** [loo-meen-AHR-ee-ahs] along the edges of these patio walls. Grandmother's friend in Northern New Mexico calls them **farolitos** [fah-roh-LEE-tohs].

Luminarias or farolitos are just about the most unusual thing I have seen in New Mexico. To make them you fill brown paper sacks with sand and put a candle in each sack. When the candles are all lit, it makes a beautiful Christmas scene.

Grandmother lights her dollhouse luminarias with tiny little bulbs instead of candles. Dollhouse matches would not be safe!

Well, now that you have seen my grandmother's adobe dollhouse, what is your favorite part?

Only a few people in New Mexico live in houses just like this. But almost every house in New Mexico has some of the things you have seen in this dollhouse.

I have never seen a shepherd's fireplace anywhere except in my grandmother's dollhouse and at a museum in Santa Fe.

But I have seen lots of beehive fireplaces in houses in New Mexico. And many people have ristras and storytellers and ollas.

I hope you can come back for a longer visit sometime. Next time let's pretend to spend the night in Grandmother's adobe dollhouse. I'm sure she would make us some tiny green chiles stuffed with cheese to eat for supper.

We could hop on the storyteller's lap for a nice long tale, and when it is time to go to sleep, we could take turns sleeping on the shepherd's fireplace!

I love to visit Grandmother in New Mexico. When it's time to leave, I take one last peek in the windows of her adobe dollhouse.

And as we drive away I say a quiet goodbye to all the adobe houses and all the special things inside. **Adios!**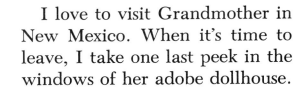

Afterword

MaryLou M. Smith is a writer, a publisher, and a fourth generation New Mexican who lives in Colorado with her husband and two children.

Her six-year-old son Matt Smith is the real little boy who gives us the tour of his grandmother's adobe dollhouse.

Grandmother is LaVerne Smith who owns a furniture store, builds dollhouses, and collects miniatures in Roswell, New Mexico. She has built and furnished several adobe dollhouses.

Ann Blackstone is an illustrator and graphic designer who inherited her love of houses from her family of architects. She lives in a 108-year-old house in Colorado with her cat, Callie.